Enhance Your Chance

Jim Whittington

FLC Business Consulting

Enhance Your Chance / Jim Whittington, 2025
Lovell Casiero, Ed.
Frances Owen, Ed.
ISBN: 979-8-9892004-2-9

Book cover and design by Frances Owen

ENHANCE YOUR CHANCE

Contents

INTRODUCTION

Enhance Your Chance is a comprehensive and transformative guide aimed at helping individuals unlock their full potential and take advantage of opportunities for success in every aspect of life. Whether your focus is on achieving personal goals, advancing in your career, or deepening your spiritual journey, this resource offers practical strategies and motivational insights designed to guide you through life's challenges and open doors to new possibilities.

Rooted in biblical wisdom, combined with actionable advice and uplifting content, *Enhance Your Chance* empowers readers to take control of their destiny and build a life that is rich in purpose, fulfillment, and abundance. For those seeking love, peace, happiness, or financial prosperity, the teachings and principles within the book offer practical applications that a diverse audience can easily adapt to enhance any area of their life.

The core message of *Enhance Your Chance* is clear: by embracing the right mindset, applying key biblical truths, and remaining persistent, readers can significantly improve their quality of life and experience blessings in ways they never imagined. No matter where you are on your journey, this guide will help you navigate toward a brighter, more prosperous future.

Chapter One

Enhance Your Chance of Winning

Winning a sweepstakes requires participation; no one has ever won without entering. Your friends may laugh at you, but someone is emerging victorious. In the race of life, sitting on the sidelines and critiquing others won't lead to victory. You must run the race to win the race. Only those who actively engage in the race have any chance at all to emerge as the winner.

If you find yourself saying, "I've tried and tried but failed repeatedly. Nothing ever works for me. I always lose., " consider that with each new attempt, your chances of success increase.

Every time you enter a race, start a new endeavor, or try to break a bad habit, you multiply your winning possibilities. Someone will triumph! Why should it not be one of God's children? Strive for success with persistence! If anyone is going to win the reward, let it be the chosen people of God who win the reward. So, never give up; try, and try again!

If you have tried to start a business and encountered financial failure ten times over, try one more time. If your marital history mirrors the woman at the well in John

4:16-18, with five unsuccessful marriages, don't despair. There is still someone out there who will love you. Give love another chance!

Ecclesiastes 9:11 in the Bible reminds us, "I have seen something else under the sun: The race is not to the swift or the battle to the strong, nor does food come to the wise or wealth to the brilliant or favor to the learned, but time and chance happen to them all." So, you see, your chances of winning are as good as anyone else, so don't give up! Keep on trying! Keep believing! Persevere!

Galatians 6:9 reinforces this sentiment, "Let us not become weary in doing good, for at the proper time we will reap a harvest if we do not give up." So, my friend, don't tire of doing what is right; your reward will come at the appointed time if you don't give up.

KEY INSIGHTS

Persistence is Key to Winning: This chapter emphasizes the importance of participation and persistence. It highlights that one cannot win a sweepstakes, race, or any endeavor in life without actively engaging in it. Sitting on the sidelines and critiquing others will not lead to victory. One must actively participate, and persistence is essential. Both increase the chances of success.

Overcoming Repeated Failures: The chapter encourages you not to lose hope despite repeated failures. It suggests that each failure is an opportunity to learn and improve, thereby enhancing the likelihood of success in future attempts. Therefore, continued effort and persistence can eventually lead to success.

Divine Encouragement and the Promise of Rewards: This chapter encourages perseverance in endeavors, especially for those who believe in God's providence. It implies that believers, as God's children, should strive with persistence, holding onto the faith that their efforts will be rewarded.

Chapter Two

ENHANCE YOUR CHANCE OF BEING HAPPY

First, you must make up your mind that you are going to be happy. Happiness is a choice, and most people are as happy as they choose to be. I once encountered a man who looked like he was having a bad day. I said to him, "Cheer up; things could be worse." He responded, "I tried that, and things did get worse." You can choose to adopt the mindset of this man, with your head cast down, dwelling on negativity, criticizing, and focusing on your trials and tribulations. Instead, why not choose to walk around with a joyful attitude, with a pep in your step, and a smile on your face? It is your choice!

No one in the Bible had more reason to be cast down than the Apostle Paul; he was beaten, chastised, and left for dead. Yet in Philippians 4:8-9, he instructs, "Finally, brothers and sisters, whatever is true, whatever is noble, whatever is right, whatever is pure, whatever is lovely, whatever is admirable – if anything is excellent or praiseworthy – think about such things. Whatever you have learned or received or heard from me or seen in me – put into practice. And the God of peace will be with you."

In Nehemiah 8:10, "Nehemiah said, "Go and enjoy choice food and sweet drinks and send some to those who have nothing prepared. This day is holy to our Lord. Do not grieve, for the joy of the Lord is your strength." Some people may be inclined to focus on negativity instead of all the blessings in their lives. You must know it is crucial to recognize that happiness is within your control.

To prove that people are pessimistic by nature, observe their media preferences. It will reveal a natural inclination towards negativity. The most popular books, podcasts, and television programs often contain significant negativity, highlighting a lack of morality, criminal activity, and sorrow. Movies with violence and killings tend to be the most popular and the most lucrative at the box office. People are naturally drawn to negative things; people will hear something bad about someone, and they'll call everyone in the world they can think of to tell them about it. When they hear good news, they tell very few people or no one at all.

The Bible says in Proverbs 23:7, "For as he thinks in his heart, so is he. "Eat and drink!" he says to you, but his heart is not with you."

Someone said that bad news will travel around the world before the good news gets out of sight. Train your thoughts to think about good things! Sometimes, when people get together, the first thing that pops into their mind is to tell them something they have heard about someone: the latest gossip. But we need to resist that temptation and say, "No, I'm going to tell them something good about someone." The quality of the visit will be increased, and you will enjoy each other's company more if you talk about the good things in life. When we do this, it brings more joy and peace to our lives, and that makes us happy.

To truly enhance your chance of being happy, remember Proverbs 3:13: "Blessed are those who find wisdom, those who gain understanding."

The Apostle Paul's letter to the Romans introduces a powerful promise: in Romans 14:22, he writes, "So whatever you believe about these things, keep between yourself and God. Blessed is the one who does not condemn himself by what he approves." If you have made mistakes, don't dwell on them; seek forgiveness, repent, and move forward.

2 Corinthians 7:10 states, "Godly sorrow brings repentance that leads to salvation and leaves no regrets." This verse further underscores that godly sorrow leads to repentance and salvation.

Romans 8:1-2 assures, "Therefore, there is now no condemnation for those who are in Christ Jesus, because through Christ Jesus the law of the Spirit who gives life has set you free from the law of sin and death."

Condemnation is a happiness thief. Reject self-condemnation, as God did not send His Son to condemn but to save[1]. Jesus promised us in John 5:24, "Very truly I tell you, whoever hears my word and believes him who sent me has eternal life and will not be judged but has crossed over from death to life."

Stand by these scriptures to eliminate condemnation because it will rob you of happiness as quickly as anything in the world. People say, "I have sinned, therefore, God won't hear my prayers. Something bad is going to happen to me because of my past deeds. The Devil is out to get me."

How many times have people told you that? You did wrong; God is going to get you for that—and then you walk around scared to death, feeling the weight of condemnation. When you try to go to sleep at night, you think, "If I die before I wake, will the Lord my soul take? I've been too bad." When you do this, you're condemning yourself again and again.

By leaning into the word of God, knowing that you have grace through Christ Jesus, and believing without a doubt that you are forgiven, you will indeed enhance your chances of being happy.

KEY INSIGHTS

Choosing Happiness: This chapter underscores the idea that happiness is a matter of choice. It contrasts the attitude of someone who prefers to dwell on negativity with the decision to adopt a joyful, positive outlook. The key takeaway is that one can consciously decide to focus on the positive aspects of life and maintain a cheerful demeanor despite challenges.

The Power of Positive Thinking and Joy in Faith: The chapter draws on biblical teachings to highlight the importance of joy and positive thinking in one's faith journey. The emphasis is on how joy and positivity are presented not just as a personal choice but as a crucial aspect of a faithful life. Focus on the good and practice maintaining a positive outlook to achieve happiness and overall well-being.

Overcoming Negativity and Condemnation: Additionally, this chapter addresses the natural human inclination towards negativity and the tendency to focus on negative news. It suggests a conscious effort to shift focus towards positive thoughts and good news. Furthermore, it delves into the biblical perspective on overcoming self-condemnation and the importance of forgiveness and repentance. Emphasizing that godly sorrow leads to salvation and freedom from condemnation, concluding with the message that by embracing forgiveness and rejecting self-condemnation, individuals can significantly enhance their happiness. Accept God's grace through Christ to achieve a more joyful and fulfilling life.

Chapter Three

Enhance Your Chance of Being Healthy

Health is a gift from God, and disregarding the laws of nature comes with consequences. I know a woman who consistently discusses her high blood pressure, yet her diet is laden with unhealthy foods that contribute to the issue. Avoid engaging in activities that harm your health. Prioritizing self-care and consuming proper nutrition are at the top of the list when it comes to being healthy. It is true; you are what you eat. Additionally, getting adequate rest and giving up bad habits that are detrimental to your overall well-being contribute significantly to how healthy you will be.

When people ask me about drinking, I offer this perspective: like many personal decisions, it is between you and God; however, if you choose to drink, practice temperance and avoid excessive consumption. Ephesians 5:18 advises, "Do not get drunk on wine, which leads to debauchery." Instead, be filled with the Spirit...

Avoid smoking altogether. If you do indulge, refrain from smoking excessively. Smoking one or two packs a day can be very harmful to your health. Many foods and substances are not good for you when consumed in large quantities. Many people drink coffee every day, but if you are going to drink coffee, don't drink ten to fifteen cups a day. Practice temperance!

The principle of temperance is highlighted in Titus 2:2: "Teach the older men to be temperate, worthy of respect, self-controlled, and sound in faith, in love, and endurance." This Bible passage emphasizes sobriety and moderation in various aspects of life, including our habits. While many focus on abstaining, the Bible teaches the value of temperance.

1 Corinthians 3:16–17, "Don't you know that you yourselves are God's temple and that God's Spirit dwells in your midst? If anyone destroys God's temple, God will destroy that person, for God's temple is sacred, and you together are that temple."

This Scripture underscores that our bodies are temples of God, urging us not to defile them. Neglecting your body affects your witness; maintaining your health enhances it. A well-cared-for body supports a vibrant testimony, devoid of bags under your eyes from lack of sleep or the impact of excessive smoking. Your witness gains more meaning when you're not struggling with the consequences of substance use. Take care of your body, and it will reciprocate; neglect it, and you will bear the cost.

KEY INSIGHTS

The Importance of Healthy Lifestyle Choices: This chapter stresses that health is a gift from God and should be treated with respect and care. Emphasizing the importance of proper nutrition, adequate rest, and the avoidance of detrimental habits as critical elements of self-care. This reinforces the idea that individual choices and habits have a direct impact on one's health and well-being.

Practicing Temperance and Moderation: The chapter offers a perspective on personal decisions such as drinking alcohol, suggesting that these choices are between the individual and God. However, it advises practicing temperance and avoiding excess in all things. The principle of temperance is portrayed as not just abstaining from certain activities but engaging in them responsibly and in moderation.

Your Body as a Temple: Drawing from 1 Corinthians 3:16–17, the chapter underscores the biblical view that the human body is a temple of God and should be treated as sacred. It teaches us that neglecting the body not only has physical consequences but also impacts one's spiritual witness. A well-cared-for body is seen as supporting a vibrant testimony and reflecting one's respect for the divine gift of health.

Chapter Four

Enhance Your Chance of Being Successful

Do you aspire to be successful? Of course you do! If not, it might be time to choose your burial attire because, without aspirations, you're akin to being lifeless already.

Success isn't solely about wealth; it's the contentment and joy derived from life's allotments. 3 John 2 expresses the desire for prosperity and health, aligning with the prosperity of the soul.

God desires your success. That said, you must consider this: success requires action.

A person who believes finding a penny is good luck must take time to stop and pick it up. I have witnessed people see a coin on the ground and not take the time to stop and pick it up. Dismissing a penny from becoming a millionaire is as distant from success as the one who refuses to pick it up. If you lack one penny being a millionaire, you are no more a millionaire than the man who refused to pick up the penny. If a journey of a thousand miles begins with one step, then the road to being a millionaire starts with one penny. Until you learn the value of a penny, you'll never know the value of a million dollars.

Recognizing the value of even the most minor opportunities is essential in the journey to success. A line from the play *Julius Caesar* by William Shakespeare validates this principle, "There is a tide in the affairs of men which, taken at the flood, leads on to fortune; omitted, all the voyage of their life is bound in shallows and in miseries."[1] Ignoring chances leads to regret and dissatisfaction. Don't miss out on opportunities while engrossed in trivial pursuits.

Sowing precedes reaping. Luke 6:38, "Give and it will be given to you. A good measure, pressed down, shaken together, and running over, will be poured into your lap. For with the measure you use, it will be measured to you." Luke's writings from the Sermon on the Mount are one of my favorite books of the Bible. The message emphasizes giving to receive, illustrating the principle that the measure you give shall be measured to you again. Plant seeds before expecting a harvest; sow abundantly to reap bountifully. God multiplies what you release. When you release it, God will increase it!

The miracles of Jesus did not happen without the recipient performing an action. Time and time again, the Bible reveals that people had to act before receiving miracles. The woman in Luke the 8th chapter touched Jesus' garment; in Mark chapter 10, Bartimaeus cried out, "Have mercy on me" and received his sight; in 2 Kings chapter 5, Naaman dipped seven times in the Jordan River to be cleansed of his leprosy. Even the rich young ruler was required to act; in Matthew 19:21, "Jesus answered, 'If you want to be perfect, go, sell your possessions and give to the poor, and you will have treasure in heaven. Then come, follow me.'" The young ruler went away sad because he was unwilling to give up such a large amount of wealth.

Are YOU willing to do what the Lord would have you do to achieve success in this life? Sometimes, the ask is complex and comes with commitment and sacrifice.

Enhance your chance of being successful by rejecting selfishness. Some people cannot stand to see anyone else succeed. They allow envy and jealousy to get in the way of being happy for others. Celebrate others' blessings authentically, and it will draw blessings toward you. If you desire a new car, praise God to the highest every time you hear someone else got a new car. I have practiced this for many years, and I promise you it works! True happiness for others brings forth genuine joy and favor.

God desires blessings for you. If you believe there's anything sacred in poverty, you're mistaken. I once thought that being poor meant closeness to God, that sickness was a form of suffering for the Lord, inferiority equated to humility, and unhappiness meant being sober-minded. However, I've come to understand that God intends to fill your life with joy, bringing a smile to your face and a sparkle to your eyes. He will lift the burdens from your shoulders, bringing victory into your life. Your eternal home will be in Heaven, where the saints become your brothers and sisters, and angels serve as your guardians. God will remove the tombstone from your hand, the coffin from your arm, unhook you from the ambulance, relocate you from the graveyard, and generously bless you and enhance your chance of success, giving your life purpose and fulfillment.

KEY INSIGHTS

Recognizing and Valuing Opportunities: This chapter emphasizes the importance of recognizing and valuing even the smallest opportunities as stepping stones to success. The penny analogy illustrates that disregarding minor opportunities can hinder the journey to achieving larger goals. It suggests that understanding the value of small gains is essential to appreciating and striving for greater achievements.

The Principle of Giving and Taking Action: The chapter underscores the biblical principle of giving to receive, as illustrated in Luke 6:38. This teaching promotes the idea that one must sow generously to reap bountifully and that God multiplies what is provided in faith. Additionally, the chapter highlights the necessity of action to achieve success, drawing on various biblical stories where miracles followed the recipient's actions. This perspective encourages proactive behavior and the willingness to make sacrifices or take steps of faith as prerequisites for experiencing success and blessings.

Rejecting Selfishness and Embracing Joy for Others: The chapter advises against envy and jealousy, promoting the practice of genuinely celebrating others' successes as a means to attract blessings. It challenges the notion that poverty, sickness, or unhappiness are inherently virtuous or indicative of closeness to God. Instead, it portrays God as desiring to fill lives with joy, purpose, and fulfillment. By finding happiness in others' achievements and rejecting selfish attitudes, individuals can enhance their chances of success and experience a more fulfilled and purpose-driven life.

Chapter Five

ENHANCE YOUR CHANCE OF HAVING PEACE

"Do not your heart be troubled," John 14:1. You can't have peaceful thoughts and fearful thoughts at the same time. If you have peaceful thoughts, there is no fear. If you have fearful thoughts, there is no peace. You should change your thinking by putting something else in your mind to replace the negative thoughts. Simultaneously harboring peaceful and fearful thoughts is impossible. Peaceful thoughts eliminate fear, and fear eliminates peace. Jesus consistently encouraged positive thinking, saying, "Be of good cheer." Despite challenges, His message was one of comfort and encouragement. Living by faith rather than emotions is essential to enhance your chance of experiencing peace.

To combat negative thoughts, you must intentionally replace them with positive alternatives. Consider the example of someone apprehensive about flying. This fear doesn't necessarily indicate a lack of faith but rather a discomfort with activities that may take you out of your comfort zone, like flying. I have also experienced anxiety about flying, dwelling on the height and the inability to exit the plane. However, I leaned into biblical principles, redirecting my thoughts towards faith and positive affirmations. The ability to shift my focus to thoughts of faith and positivity replaced the initial feelings of anxiety and fear, making my flights more enjoyable. Replacing apprehensive thoughts with thoughts of peace became a transformative practice.

The way to get rid of thoughts of fear is to replace them with thoughts of faith. This is something you must learn and train your mind to think differently. To overcome fearful thoughts, one must intentionally replace them with thoughts of faith. This is a learned skill that requires practice, often with the guidance of spiritual leaders in the church, such as teachers, evangelists, prophets, apostles, and pastors. Feeding your soul with spiritual books, listening to uplifting messages, attending church services, and participating in daily practice of prayer and meditation are ways to reinforce positive thinking and strengthen your faith.

When I was first starting as a young preacher, another preacher and spiritual mentor invited me to his home. His library of books was extensive, and he emphasized the transformative power of reading inspirational books. He asked me how many books I thought he had in the library. I said, "I'm not sure, but there must be thousands." He said, "I have not read all the books in this library, but I've read something from every book. How many hours do you think I might have put in reading these books?" I said, "I couldn't guess. I wouldn't know where to start."

He walked over to his desk and picked up a stack of books about twelve inches high—seven or eight books. He told me, "I bought all the books in this library and read from them looking for these. If you don't have them, go buy them and read them; they will change your life." I made a list of the books and went out and bought the ones that I didn't have, and they did change my life. He urged me to read these specific titles that had profoundly impacted his life, as he knew they would change mine as well.

Reading various self-help books and realizing their frequent references to biblical scriptures reinforced the importance of turning to the Bible for guidance and strength. The more I invested time in reading books on happiness, overcoming fear, positive thinking, and the power of prayer, the more it proved instrumental in transforming my perspective. It was not long into this practice that I realized the fear that was robbing me of my peace was replaced by a deeper trust in God's promises.

Jesus was a positive thinker. Everywhere He went, He said, "Be of good cheer."[1] Most people you ask can tell you ten things wrong with them. But Jesus said, "Be of good cheer," and He never asked anyone how they felt; He just told them, "Be of good cheer, be of good comfort, be not afraid." You will never enhance your chance of having peace if you go by your feelings. You must live by your faith.

Read your Bible. You'll find help there; you'll find strength there. Replace your thoughts with peaceful thoughts—happy thoughts, and ultimately, you will have peace beyond all understanding. John 14:27, "Peace I leave with you; my peace I give you; I do not give to you as the world gives. Do not let your hearts be troubled and do not be afraid." The Prophet Isaiah confirms that we only need to trust in God to access peace. Isaiah 26:3 says, "You will keep in perfect peace those whose minds are steadfast, because they trust in you."

KEY INSIGHTS

Replace Fearful Thoughts with Peaceful Ones: It's impossible to hold peaceful and fearful thoughts simultaneously. To achieve peace, one must consciously replace negative thoughts with positive and faith-based thoughts. This practice requires intentionality and consistency and is often supported by spiritual activities such as prayer, reading uplifting literature, and meditating on positive affirmations.

The Role of Faith in Overcoming Fear: Living by faith rather than emotions is crucial for maintaining peace. Jesus emphasized the importance of positive thinking and faith, frequently encouraging His followers to "be of good cheer" and not to be afraid. Trusting in God's promises and focusing on faith can transform anxiety and fear into peace and comfort.

The Transformative Power of Spiritual Guidance and Reading: Engaging with spiritual mentors, reading inspirational books, and immersing oneself in the Bible can significantly enhance one's ability to maintain peace. The wisdom and encouragement found in these resources reinforce positive thinking and help replace fearful thoughts with faith and peace. As illustrated by the author's experience, reading and applying the teachings from these books can lead to a profound shift in perspective and a deeper sense of peace.

Chapter Six

ENHANCE YOUR CHANCE OF BEING REMEMBERED WHEN YOUR LIFE IS OVER

L et's face the truth! It is natural to want people to remember you after your time on this earth is over. The thought of not being remembered is daunting. God help us if we were to die, and no one would remember us or miss us. Our legacy isn't just about who we were, but we are also remembered for what we accomplished in our lifetime, for our good works, and for the impact we have on others.

The Bible emphasizes this human inclination to be remembered even beyond our lifetime. Psalm 49:10-11, "For all can see that the wise die, that the foolish and the senseless also perish, leaving their wealth to others. Their tombs will remain their houses forever, their dwellings for endless generations, though they had named lands after themselves."

This Psalm proves that man wants to be remembered, even after he is gone. We name streets, boulevards, buildings, schools, parks, and other public places after people who have made a mark in history so they will be remembered.

However, being remembered isn't solely about our names but about our deeds. Take, for instance, historical figures like John F. Kennedy. If John F. Kennedy had never been a US Senator or President of the United States, you might ask, "Who was he?" when I mentioned his name.

As the 16th President of the United States, Abraham Lincoln signed the Emancipation Proclamation.[1] He is remembered not only as a United States president but also because one act during his presidency had an impact on a nation, and many people benefited from his decision.

Over and over, history teaches us that people are remembered not just for their names but for the impact they had during their lives. Legendary entertainers are indeed remembered for the greatness they achieved in their genre of art, music, or literature, for example. William Shakespeare, the English playwright and poet, died in 1616, but his literary works live on today in books and plays over 400 years later.

Celebrities come and go, but some leave the legacy of their name behind them. Perhaps they had become legends, some in their own time. People name their children after them. Their children are not legends, but they are named after a legend. Maybe they think this will give their child an advantage in life if they name them after someone great.

Your legacy extends to your children and grandchildren. In Proverbs, the Bible reminds us of the significance of being remembered through generations. Proverbs 17:6, "Children's children are a crown to the aged, and the parents are the pride of their children." If you're a grandfather or great-grandfather, your descendants become a testament to your influence and your works. To every parent, grandparent, and great-grandparent reading this, you have a crown. Your children and grandchildren will remember you. Ensure that you are leaving a positive influence on them so they will be a positive reflection of your legacy. Raise them in a Godly home, teach them to pray and trust in the Lord. Be a shining example to them of a life built on love and faith.

To be remembered even by those closest to you, you have to do something. If you just carry your name around, you're relying on reflected glory. You're like the moon—you're just a reflection of the sun. You have no light of your own. To have a lasting impact, it's crucial to do something noteworthy in your own name, creating a mark that will endure.

You can leave your mark even in the simplest of ways. Plant a tree, teach a child, write something, record something, build something, and you will be remembered long after you are gone because you left something tangible that came from the works of your hands.

The legacy you leave matters, and to ensure it is one you want to be remembered by and one you can be proud of, you must be authentic, strive for excellence, and show kindness to the people you encounter.

Some people do things just to be remembered, lacking authenticity. Some even do negative things, which some people refer to as "their fifteen minutes of fame." They assassinate a leader, bomb buildings, or even blow themselves up like terrorists. They do these kinds of things only to be remembered; however, they are remembered negatively and horribly.

Maya Angelo said, "I've learned that people will forget what you said, people will forget what you did, but people will never forget how you made them feel."[2] Go out of your way to be a blessing to those you encounter. Say something or do something that will bring them joy and make them feel good. Lift them up, and they will remember you and share a testament of the impact your kindness had on them.

KEY INSIGHTS

Impact Through Actions and Accomplishments: People are remembered not merely by their names but by the significant actions and accomplishments they achieved during their lifetime. Historical figures like Abraham Lincoln and John F. Kennedy are remembered for their impactful deeds, such as signing the Emancipation Proclamation or leading the country. Engaging in meaningful actions and contributing positively to society ensures a lasting legacy.

Creating a Tangible Legacy: Leaving a tangible mark through simple actions can ensure you are remembered. Planting a tree, teaching a child, writing, recording, or building something are examples of how one can leave behind something enduring. These acts create a lasting impression and serve as a testament to one's efforts and contributions.

Positive Influence on Future Generations: Your legacy extends to your children and grandchildren. Proverbs 17:6 highlights the importance of being remembered through generations. By raising children in a Godly home, teaching them to pray, and being a positive example, you can ensure your values and influence are carried forward. Authenticity, striving for excellence, and showing kindness are crucial for leaving a legacy that your descendants will be proud of and remember fondly.

Chapter Seven

ENHANCE YOUR CHANCE OF A GOOD NIGHT'S REST

P salm 4:8 states, "In peace I will both lie down and sleep, for you alone, Lord, make me dwell in safety."

It's astonishing how many people struggle to find rest at night. If you're facing sleep troubles, there's a guaranteed method that doesn't involve sleeping pills or other remedies. You must first decide if there is something specific that is keeping you from sleeping. Perhaps you have something on your mind, you have pain in your body, or there is noise. It may be as simple as removing the distraction.

When the devil attempts to disrupt your peace and keep you awake, counteract it by praying for everyone who comes to your mind. Some people think you need to be on your knees to pray, but you don't even need to get out of bed; you should just sincerely offer prayers to those individuals. Whether it's your children, friends, or anyone else on your mind, lift them up in prayer. The Devil would rather you sleep than engage in powerful prayer. Just pray, "God, whatever they need, give it to them, protect them, guide them, bless them." The person that comes to your mind for prayer may be going through something you do not even know about, but God knows. As you continue to pray, others will come to your mind; pray for them. Additionally, turning your mind to prayer for others removes any worry or anxiety plaguing your thoughts that may keep you from a peaceful sleep.

Allow me to share a personal experience. I used to have two bulldogs. Their names were Amos and Andy. The one named Andy could escape from anything. I should have named him Houdini. Very often, they would disturb my sleep by barking. Frustrated, I would lie there wishing they would stop, and sometimes I even prayed for them to stop. Then, a revelation came to me – instead of praying, why not get up and tell them to stop? Often, our prayers stem from laziness, expecting God to act on our behalf. In this case, I needed to address the issue myself, and once I did, the dogs remained silent.

You've heard it said many times throughout your life that prayer changes things. I want to take that one step further: prayer changes people, and people change things. I lay there wishing the dogs would stop barking, even praying they would. But when I received a word of wisdom from God, it became clear to me that I just needed to act! Why didn't I get up and tell them to stop barking? To be honest, the way I handled it was a form of laziness. A lot of the prayers we pray are because we are too lazy to do anything about it ourselves. We want God to do it for us. Our lack of participation is hindering change in our circumstances.

On another occasion, I prayed for a man who was asking God to give him a better car. I believed that God had heard my prayer. I was so elated that I immediately prophesied to him. I told him, "God is going to give you a better car." Days and weeks went by, and nothing happened. He did not get a car, so I bought a car and gave it to him. Truth be told, I could have saved time by skipping the praying and prophesying and simply doing what I knew God wanted me to do from the beginning. Sometimes, we argue with God or pretend we are not receiving what He would have us do in service of others. You see, this man was an older minister, and he had been serving God and his people for a long time. I knew God wanted me to be the conduit of how he got a better car, but I was resisting. Sometimes, sleep may not come because you are like Jacob in the Bible: you are wrestling with God or a decision in your life. That is when you have to dig deep, put your faith to work, pray for discernment, and trust God.

I hope the stories I've shared illustrate the importance of not praying for things we're unwilling to act upon. If you're not prepared to play a role in seeking a solution to your problem or achieving that thing you are asking God for, think twice before uttering it. You also need to recognize that God does not always answer your prayer like you want Him to because He knows what is best for you.

Lastly, take proactive steps to address the factors that disturb your sleep before closing your eyes. Put your phone down at least an hour before you go to bed, turn off your television, and avoid eating a heavy meal late in the evening. Spend the last hour of your evening in prayer and meditation. Preparing your mind, body, and environment for a peaceful night's rest will enhance your chance of a good night's rest.

KEY INSIGHTS

Proactive Problem Solving and Personal Responsibility: Identify specific factors that disturb your sleep and take proactive steps to address them. This could include removing distractions, such as noise or physical discomfort, and directly dealing with issues that can be solved by personal action. For instance, rather than simply praying for a solution, actively engage in resolving the problem yourself, as illustrated by the author's experience with his barking dogs.

The Power of Prayer for Others: When sleep eludes you, use the time to pray for others rather than focus on your own restlessness. By lifting others in prayer, you can transform the negative experience of sleeplessness into a spiritually productive one. This practice not only helps you find peace but also shifts your focus from personal anxiety to compassion and intercession for others' needs.

Preparation and Environment for Rest: Prepare your mind, body, and environment to enhance your chance of a good night's rest. Establish a bedtime routine that includes turning off electronic devices, avoiding heavy meals, and engaging in prayer and meditation. Creating a calm and conducive environment for sleep can significantly improve your ability to rest peacefully, aligning with the biblical promise of dwelling in safety and peace.

Chapter Eight

Enhance Your Chance of Having Successful Relationships

I have often said you don't choose the people you love or the people who love you. God does that for you. Usually, people come together in a relationship, be it a friendship, marriage, or family relationship, and their personalities can be so different from one another. Yet they form a bond of love and caring for one another. Have you ever wondered why some friendships last for years and others only last for a time and season?

Achieving success in a relationship requires selflessness. You need to be willing to put the needs of someone else before your own. This is easier said than done. In the book of Matthew, Jesus gave us two commandments: "Love the Lord your God with all your heart and with all your soul and with all your mind." This is the first and greatest commandment. And the second is like it: "Love your neighbor as yourself." All the Law and the Prophets hang on these two commandments.[1]

Jesus's teachings on love extend beyond mere feelings. He instructs us to love others as we love ourselves, not more, not less. The depth of your love for another is not confined to your heart but is manifested through your actions. As my mother used to say, "Love in actions, not in words." You can profess your love multiple times a day, but if your actions lack care, kindness, and empathy, you're not contributing to the relationship.

Do you know what the primary cause of divorce is? It's not about blaming individuals, whether they are considered good or bad. Accusations are often made against women for supposedly 'taking' husbands or against men for allegedly 'taking' someone else's wife. The reality is that you can't 'take' anybody's spouse. If someone can be 'taken,' they weren't yours to begin with. I believe that if someone can 'take' your spouse, then let them, and I think that God will put someone in your life who they can't 'take.' Author Richard Bach wrote in his inspirational book Jonathan Livingston Seagull, "If you love something, set it free. If it comes back to you, it's yours. If it doesn't, it never was."[2]

Contrary to popular belief, the leading cause of divorce is not financial issues—it's the lack of communication. When communication breaks down in relationships, be it marriage, friends, co-workers, or children, the bond is at risk. Lack of communication creates problems, but communication plagued with negativity is equally devastating to your relationships.

A man I know had a wife who threatened to leave him daily, causing him to invest nothing emotionally. Relationships require investing emotionally, not to be confused with excitement. Day after day, the threat of abandonment was like a dark cloud hovering over the relationship. One day, he reminded her that leaving was a two-way street, but even that did not stop her threats. Eventually, he left, and they never lived together again. Their fear of opening up prevented a more profound connection, hindering genuine emotions and eventually destroying the marriage.

Think back to the first few months of a relationship. Conversations between a couple dating flow so easily. You want to know everything about each other, and you genuinely care about how each other's day was. Today, real conversation has been replaced with screen time. Between the phone, computer, and television, there is very little time for face-to-face conversations. If this is your lot, I encourage you to be intentional about making time for personal contact and conversations.

Positive and frequent communication is essential in any relationship, even with co-workers and employees. The importance of such matters manifests itself during our travels across the United States, where we have church services and meetings with our prayer partners. A meeting in a convention center requires a team of people. We all travel together on tour buses. Often, when someone starts pulling away and stops communicating, it won't be long until they'll be leaving us. Lack of communication is a silent force that separates more people than any other factor. Someone once said that a person does not leave their job; they leave their boss. People do not like to be kept in the dark. Lack of communication in the workplace creates a lack of trust between the employer and employee. Great leaders are great communicators.

Friendship is not essential to life; it is not valued for usefulness, but it is an extraordinary gift to have a true friend. Authentic friendship does not impose expectations on the other person. The beauty of friendship is found in the beauty of two people who share the same truths, implore the same values, and have a mutual recognition of views, ideas, and moral principles. The friendship deepens as they share experiences and explore truths together. The closest friends grow together in their beliefs. Friendship is a gift that enriches your life, and you must be a good friend to experience the blessing of true friendship.

Saying, "No one will make a fool out of me," may hold you back from happiness. Taking chances in life is crucial. If someone is going to make a fool out of you, discovering it sooner is better. God will provide someone who will love you and care for you rather than try to hurt you and tear you down. Faithfulness to others is a matter of the heart, beyond your control.

In more than sixty years of preaching and through my personal experiences, I have found that people are afraid to let their guard down, fearful of getting hurt. Many individuals fear being vulnerable, so they guard their hearts. They hesitate to invest emotionally, worried about their hearts being broken. You need to open up your heart even if it means a bit of hurt may come in. To love at all is to be vulnerable; opening up exposes us to being hurt. To close off the heart from pain can isolate any form of true love and cause you to miss out on one of the best experiences of life. To refuse to love and be loved can cause a person to become hardened and insensitive to others. Open your heart! If it doesn't prove anything else, it will prove that at least you're still alive.

In relationships, it's crucial to take a chance on love and embrace vulnerability rather than live in fear and miss out on the experience. If you are struggling in a relationship, I invite you first to look inward and ask what you need to change. That said, you also need to be realistic about whether the other person in the relationship is willing to meet you in the middle. You cannot make a person love you or be faithful to you. You cannot make them communicate with you. You cannot make them open up their heart, but God can, and He does when He joins two people together in marriage, friendship, and family. 1 John 4:7: "Dear friends, let us love one another, for love comes from God. Everyone who loves has been born of God and knows God."

God has the power to change many aspects of your life, except your attitude; that's a change you must make yourself. If you tend to be sarcastic or short with the people in your sphere, it's on you to change. If you are challenged with patience or under much stress, you may find yourself snapping back at your spouse or your children over the most minor things. You will become a better person if you learn to manage that trait. My mother used to say, "You can get more bees with honey than you can with vinegar." God won't intervene in changing your attitude, but He gives you the tools to change if you really desire change to become a better person. "But the fruit of the Spirit is love, joy, peace, forbearance, kindness, goodness, faithfulness, gentleness and self-control."[3]

In any relationship, you need to leave your ego at the door. Wayne Dyer said that ego is edging God out.[4] If you often worry about what type of impression you are making on people, you will improve your relationships by stopping the worry about how others perceive you. By taking this approach, it will create a version of you that is more genuine and less calculated. By placing less emphasis on what others think of you, you will present a more authentic version of yourself. Openness and vulnerability are meaningful to the success of human relations. The Apostle Paul teaches us, "As a prisoner for the Lord then, I urge you to live a life worthy of the calling you have received. Be completely humble and gentle; be patient, bearing with one another in love. Make every effort to keep the unity of the Spirit through the bond of peace."[5]

Finally, the most important relationship is a relationship with God. Without a relationship with God, you are not spiritually whole. Until you have found inner peace and happiness in your spiritual journey, it will be challenging to have a solid relationship with others. As referenced earlier in this chapter, this is the first commandment, "Love the Lord your God with all your heart and with all your soul and with all your mind." The second and another important part of this commandment is "Love your neighbor as yourself."[6] I want to emphasize the importance of self-love. It is often the hardest of all. However, by not showing yourself love, grace, and self-care, you are not setting yourself up to be a person who will genuinely be able to love others. Reread the verse and pay close attention to the word 'as.' Jesus does not teach us to love others more or less than ourselves but equally to ourselves. Can you give yourself enough grace to show the same love to you as you show to others?

KEY INSIGHTS

Selflessness and Genuine Actions: Successful relationships require selflessness and putting the needs of others before your own. Genuine love is demonstrated through actions rather than words. Jesus' command to love others as yourself emphasizes the importance of care, kindness, and empathy in relationships. This selfless love strengthens bonds and fosters lasting connections.

Communication and Vulnerability: Open, honest, and positive communication is essential for maintaining healthy relationships. Lack of communication or negative interactions can lead to misunderstandings and separation. Embracing vulnerability and being willing to open your heart despite the risk of hurt is crucial. This openness allows for deeper connections and prevents the isolation that comes from guarding your emotions.

Personal Responsibility and Growth: Building successful relationships involves personal responsibility and continuous self-improvement. You must work on your attitude and behavior, managing traits like impatience or stress that can negatively impact your interactions. Leaving your ego at the door and presenting a genuine, less calculated version of yourself helps in forming authentic and meaningful connections. Additionally, the foundation of all relationships is a strong relationship with God, as spiritual wholeness enhances your ability to relate to and love others effectively.

Chapter Nine

ENHANCE YOUR CHANCE OF BEING SAVED

Salvation is not attained by wishing you were saved. You cannot wish your way into Heaven, and you will never be saved by simply wanting to be better. Heaven is not attained through a mere longing to be better or attempting to improve yourself. You cannot secure salvation merely by wishing or desiring it.

Salvation is achieved by placing your belief in the Lord Jesus Christ, confessing your sins, repenting, and openly acknowledging that Jesus is the Lord of your life. Romans 10:9 affirms this, stating, "If you declare with your mouth, 'Jesus is Lord,' and believe in your heart that God raised him from the dead, you will be saved."

When the Philippian jailer fell trembling before the Apostle Paul and Silas, asking, "Sirs, what must I do to be saved?" They replied, "Believe in the Lord Jesus, and you will be saved –- you and your household."[1] Further, the Apostle Paul also teaches us in Ephesians 2:8-10, "For it is by grace you have been saved, through faith — and this is not from yourselves, it is the gift of God — not by works, so that no one can boast." We are God's handiwork, created in Christ Jesus to do good works, which God prepared in advance for us to do.

When the Apostle Peter preached the sermon on the Day of Pentecost, he said in Acts 2:38-39, "Repent and be baptized, every one of you, in the name of Jesus Christ for the forgiveness of your sins. And you shall receive the gift of the Holy Spirit. The promise is for you and your children, and for all who are far off — for all whom the Lord our God will call."

There are two points I want to highlight in these biblical messages. The first is that the Apostle Paul told the jailer that not only would his belief attain salvation for himself, but he also declared the same salvation would be afforded to his household. Peter also affirms this in his sermon on the day of Pentecost. Do you have people in your house you would like to see saved? Do you have children that have strayed away from the faith-based upbringing you gave them? As you confess your sins and your beliefs, so shall they be saved also!

The second point that you need to understand is that your good deeds will not give you eternal life. The Bible teaches us in Titus chapter 3 that when God's kindness and love appeared, it was not because of the works of righteousness the people had done but according to His mercy. This is why you must confess you are a sinner and ask for forgiveness so that God's mercies will be upon you.

This is how you enhance your chance of attaining salvation and securing an eternal reward: repent, believe, and confess. The rest will fall into place. As stated in I John 1:7, "But if we walk in the light, as he is in the light, we have fellowship with one another, and the blood of Jesus, his Son purifies us from all sin."

Salvation will come when you replace wishing and trying with believing and confessing that Jesus died for you and knowing that His blood washes all your sins away. Hebrews 9:22, "In fact, according to the Law, practically every purification takes place by means of blood; and if there is no shedding of blood, there is no remission."

There is no sin too big or too bad that the grace from Calvary does not redeem it. There is no one so lost that God cannot bring them into the kingdom and use them. God turned a shepherd into a king; before Paul was an Apostle for Christ, he was a persecutor and murderer of Christians. Jesus called 12 simple fishermen to fishers of men and made them the foundation of the church.

Our meeting in Heaven is assured because we have been redeemed at a price. The lyrics of a hymn of old echo the sentiment:[2]

"He paid a debt He did not owe;
I owed a debt I could not pay.
I needed someone to wash my sins away.
And now I sing a brand-new song, it's Amazing Grace.
Christ Jesus paid the debt that I could never pay."

If you have never confessed and repented of your sins, if you have never confessed your belief that Jesus died for your sins, that He shed his blood on Calvary, that you can be saved by grace, it is not too late. Say these words out loud right now.

Lord, I am a sinner.

I come to you today confessing my sins and asking for forgiveness.

I believe that you sent your Son, Jesus, into the world to live among your people.

I believe He was crucified and died at Calvary.

I believe He rose again on the third day.

And I believe the blood He shed at Calvary covers my sins, and I am redeemed.

I believe that He will also save my household.

Amen, Lord. I accept this in the name of your Son, Jesus.

KEY INSIGHTS

Salvation Through Faith and Confession: Salvation cannot be attained by merely wishing for or desiring it. It requires placing your belief in Jesus Christ, confessing your sins, repenting, and openly acknowledging Jesus as the Lord of your life. Romans 10:9 underscores this, emphasizing the importance of declaring Jesus as Lord and believing in His resurrection for salvation.

The Role of Grace and Mercy: Salvation is not earned through good deeds or works of righteousness but is a gift from God through His grace and mercy. Ephesians 2:8-10 and Titus 3 highlight that it is by God's mercy, not our actions, that we are saved. This underscores the necessity of confessing sins and seeking forgiveness to receive God's mercy and salvation.

The Promise of Salvation for You and Your Household: The Bible teaches that faith in Jesus Christ can lead to the salvation of not only the individual but also their household. Acts 16:31 and Acts 2:38-39 affirm that believing in Jesus and repenting can extend salvation to one's family. This encourages believers to have faith that their loved ones can also be saved through their example and God's promise.

Chapter Ten

Enhance Your Chance of Living a Longer Life

The desire for a longer life is universal, and gaining wisdom from those who have lived through the years is invaluable. When I meet an older person, I like to sit down and ask them questions.

My great uncle, Reverend H. L. Whittington, reached the remarkable age of 103. In his later years, after the passing of his wife, he married a woman twenty-five years his junior and continued to live a joyful and fulfilling life. When he was in his 90s, he still drove his car and still preached. During this time, I asked him, "Uncle Harry, what is your secret of a long life? How have you lived to be as old as you are?"

When asked about the secret to his longevity, Uncle Harry shared two principles. Firstly, he emphasized the importance of staying engaged in meaningful projects. He said, "I'm always in a project, always building a church or helping to remodel a church. I've always got something to do." Continually involved in building and remodeling churches, he completed a remarkable 31 building and renovation projects throughout his ministry. Uncle Harry said, "If I ever pause, God may call me home before my time. God might look over the portals of Heaven and say, 'Well, he's not doing anything—bring him on home.'"

Secondly, he surrounded himself with youthful-acting people who exuded energy, regardless of their actual age. Uncle Harry said, "I never sit around with people who just sit in rocking chairs and talk about the good old days." He said, "I surround myself with young people – or at least people who think young." Rather than reminiscing solely about the past, he engaged with those who thought young and lived in the present.

My uncle believed age is a state of mind, and you can be 75 yet think and feel young. I have some friends who are in their 50s and 60s, but when you talk to them, they talk like they're in their 30s. They are just beginning to live. It's all right to know about the good old days, and it's all right to think about them occasionally, but don't live in them. Get up—go out and do something!

Remember this: if you are living in the past, you are likely depressed; if you are living in the future, you may be experiencing anxiety. Neither of these symptoms promotes good health. So, live in the moment and make the most of each moment.

My advice to living a long life includes staying active, surrounding yourself with a positive environment, and not lingering in the past. Reflect on Uncle Harry's example. Even when faced with the loss of a loved one, Uncle Harry advocated for moving forward in life, carrying the memory of his time with Aunt Lydia with love and peace.

A dear friend once told me that to be long-lived, "You must have something to do, something to look forward to, and someone to love." Once I heard this advice, I started striving to follow it in all aspects of my life.

It's common to keep little mementos, little relics from the past, or from a family member or friend who passed away. I went into a preacher's home who had been sick for a long time. It didn't seem like he could get better. His wife was collecting mementos of a famous entertainer who had passed away. I said to him, "Brother, I believe one of the reasons you can't get healed is you're surrounded by death. On every wall, there is a picture, there's a statue, there's a relic. They are all memories of a dead man." Mementos and relics from the past should not trap you in a dwelling of death, as God is the God of the living. Jesus said in Luke 20:38, "For He is not the God of the dead, but of the living, for to Him all are alive."

I've questioned the loss of a loved one and wondered why it happened. I wondered why God would take someone I loved. Every time I buried one of my loved ones, I felt like a piece of me was buried with them as I got a little older. But I can tell you from my own experience you will smile again!

I remember the day we buried my sister, Millie, and her little girl, Sharon, who were both killed in an automobile wreck by a drunk driver. Standing by the graveside with my family, weeping as we watched my sister's coffin being lowered into the ground and her daughter, Sharon, beside her—I looked at my mother. I thought, "Momma, we'll never smile again. It's over. There will never be another happy day in our lives. This is too much to bear; we will never recover from this tragedy."

That loved one whom you have loved for so long and who is gone now wants you to be happy. Don't sit around weeping. Your tears of sorrow do not bless them; they are blessed by seeing you happy as they look down from above. If they see us happy, they are happy!

A friend from Los Angeles, who is a psychiatrist, listened as I shared with him what I am sharing with you now, and he wept. He said, "I've been needing to hear something like this for many years." Grief affects people in all walks of life. I didn't understand why my little niece, Sharon, never had a chance to grow up. One night, as I started to walk into a crusade, still feeling the hurt and pain of loss, I felt my sister by my side just as real as I did on the days we would walk to school together. I could hear her say, "Jimmy, go and keep on preaching. We're okay, we are with Jesus."

This personal experience of loss prompted me to realize that remembering loved ones in a positive light allows for healing and the continuation of life. Choosing to smile again and live amongst the living, rather than dwelling in grief, leads to a fuller and longer life.

Last but certainly not least, you must have a relationship with God, and your faithfulness will increase your years. The Book of Job tells the story of a man who was faithful to God in all things. He was so devout and dedicated to God that the Devil wanted to break him. Job lost everything, his children, his wealth, and even his health. His wife told him he should curse God and die. But Job remained faithful, and in Job 5:26, God affirms, "You will come to the grave in full vigor, like sheaves gathered in full season." It is said that Job lived 210 years, and 140 years of them were after he was tested, tried, and proved his faithfulness to God. Job was faithful to God, and in return, God was loyal to him. He restored everything he lost, and his years on earth were long, just as God promised. It is also said that the whole world mourned Job's death.[1]

The verse of one of my favorite songs says it all.

Great is Thy faithfulness
Great is Thy faithfulness
Morning by morning, new mercies I see
All I have needed Thy hand hath provided
Great is Thy faithfulness, Lord, unto me[2]

I leave you with this: Live in the present, stay busy, and be faithful to God. Many verses in the Bible speak to longevity and the promise of a long life. When life tries to keep you in a state of grief, remembering a painful past, or anxious about the future, think about these scriptures and be encouraged that you can live a long and full life and leave a legacy that your family and friends will remember fondly.

Over and over, the Bible promises a long life.

Psalm 91:16, "With long life will I satisfy him, and show him my salvation."

Psalm 103:5 further assures, "Who satisfies your desires with good things so that your youth is renewed like the eagle's."

Proverbs 3:2 adds, "For they will prolong your life many years and bring you peace and prosperity."

KEY INSIGHTS

Stay Active and Engaged:
Keeping busy with meaningful projects and activities is crucial for longevity. Reverend H.L. Whittington attributed his long life to always having something to do, such as building or remodeling churches. Staying engaged in purposeful activities keeps the mind and body active and prevents feelings of aimlessness that can lead to decline.

Surround Yourself with Positive, Youthful Energy:
Associating with positive, energetic people who think young can significantly impact your outlook on life. Uncle Harry avoided spending time with those who only reminisced about the past and instead engaged with forward-thinking and active individuals. This mindset helps maintain a youthful spirit and a positive attitude, which is essential for a long and fulfilling life.

Live in the Present and Foster Positive Relationships:
Living in the present moment, rather than dwelling on the past or worrying about the future, promotes mental well-being and good health. The advice to have something to do, something to look forward to, and someone to love underscores the importance of meaningful relationships and activities. Additionally, a strong relationship with God and faithfulness can contribute to a longer life, as exemplified by the story of Job, whose faithfulness was rewarded with longevity and restoration.

Chapter Eleven

Enhance Your Chance of Being Loved

"A friend loves at all times." Proverbs 17:17 and John 3:16 remind us of God's unparalleled love and sacrifice, stating, "For God so loved the world that he gave his one and only Son, that whosoever believes in him should not perish, but have everlasting life."

Additionally, Solomon beautifully portrays love's strength, comparing it to the intensity of death and the cruelty of jealousy. "Place me as a seal over your heart, like a seal on your arm, for love is as strong as death, its jealousy unyielding as the grave. It burns like a blazing fire, like a mighty flame."[1]

You can enhance your chance of being loved by opening up and being willing to love unconditionally. In the words of Oscar Hammerstein II, lyricist and author, "A bell is not a bell until you ring it. A song is not a song until you sing it. Love in your heart wasn't put there to stay, and love isn't love until you give it away."[2]

Proverbs 18:24 wisely advises, "One who has unreliable friends soon comes to ruin, but there is a friend who sticks closer than a brother." The cross symbolizes the greatest expression of love in the universe. To enhance your chance of being loved, open your heart and give love to someone else. Holding love within is an act of selfishness. Love is not something you talk about; love is something you do! It's about the small, everyday actions that show your love and commitment, and in doing so, you will find a deep sense of fulfillment and joy.

Love's presence is its reward; its absence is its punishment. No one can be happy without being loved. And no man is unhappy if he is in love. Richness is found in love, and poverty is absent where love prevails.

The atmosphere created by two individuals in love is palpable. Witnessing a couple in the throes of love at a gathering, radiating joy and warmth, is a testament to the transformative power of love. It inspires hope and a belief in the possibility of such love in our own lives. A couple in love will light up the room simply because they are in love. When you are around them, you feel good by just being in their presence. They demonstrate love by holding hands, touching, and maybe a simple glance, but every second, you are aware that they are in love. This is not the superficiality of lust, but the depth of genuine love expressed through touches, glances, and shared moments.

Jesus teaches the importance of touch in love in Mark 16:18, "they will place their hands on sick people, and they will get well." That touch is love. God is love and the ultimate healer. Love will heal you, but hate will kill you. Love fosters beauty, while hatred breeds ugliness. Grudges and hatred can mar a person's countenance, turning them into a reflection of the bitterness within.

I am sure you have met a couple who may have seemed the most unlikely to find each other, but who have vowed to spend the rest of their lives together. Love comes from the heart and not the physical appearance. Beauty is not only in the eye of the beholder, but it is in the heart of the beheld. The connection between love and physical appearance is evident, but love is a transformative force that transcends physical appearances.

To me, one of the prettiest women I've ever known is my mother. The unconditional love she had for me was why I saw everything beautiful when I looked at her. She was my momma, and she loved me even when I was wrong. When I couldn't help myself, momma helped me. When I couldn't feed myself, momma fed me. When I couldn't change my clothes, momma did. When I couldn't wash my face, momma washed me. If you look at your mother today and you think she's old-fashioned, look one more time. You'll see a beauty there that the world can't duplicate. True beauty does not conform to societal beauty norms; beauty comes through the love a person embodies.

You can take a man to court and make him support his wife and children, but you can't make him love them. Only God can do that. Legal obligations may secure financial support, but love is beyond legal mandates. Genuine love is a divine gift, not acquired through teaching, learning, or inheritance. It cannot be purchased; it is a gift.

I invite you to pray this simple prayer every day, "Lord, baptize me in the Love of God. Let it flow like a river through me. Teach me to love others as I love myself. Amen!"

In conclusion, to enhance your chance of being loved, embrace love's transformative power. Demonstrate love through actions, cherish meaningful connections, and let the love of God radiate through your life. Love can elevate, heal, and beautify, making it an essential element for a fulfilling and enriched existence.

KEY INSIGHTS

Love Requires Openness and Action: To be loved, you must open your heart and give love unconditionally. Love is not meant to be held within but shared through actions. Proverbs 18:24 highlights the importance of friendliness and genuine connections. Love is demonstrated through small, everyday acts of kindness, care, and commitment, which cultivate a sense of fulfillment and joy.

The Transformative Power of Love: Love has the power to transform lives, create beauty, and heal. Its presence is rewarding and enriching, while its absence brings unhappiness. Love fosters positive energy and inspiration, evident in the palpable atmosphere created by two individuals in love. Genuine love transcends physical appearances and societal norms, as seen in the deep connections between loved ones, such as a mother's unconditional love for her child.

Divine Love and Its Healing Power: True love is a sacred gift that cannot be acquired through legal means, teaching, or purchase. It is a gift from God that enhances one's chance of being loved. Praying for God's love to flow through you and embracing His teachings on love, as illustrated in Mark 16:18 and John 3:16, allows you to embody and share this transformative love. This divine love elevates, heals, and beautifies, making it essential for a fulfilling and enriched life.

Chapter Twelve

ENHANCE YOUR CHANCE RIGHT NOW

The advantage that you and I have in this world is that we have help from unseen and unexpected sources. A vast portion of the world remains unaware of the potent force that accompanies having God as our ally. I am convinced that starting from this moment, God is going to enhance your chance to be happy, prosperous, healthy, loving, kind, peaceful, and all the other steps we have talked about in this book. This divine support has the power to transform your life in ways you never thought possible.

When faced with decisions, livelihood pursuits, the search for a husband or wife, and life-changing decisions—when confronted with the demands and expectations of life—many are oblivious to the significance of having God support them. Having God on your side significantly enhances your chances of manifesting well-being and peace of mind, having all your needs met, supplies available, and your household saved.

I would choose God over the backing of the most prominent advertising agencies in New York, London, or any other city. I would prefer God over the endorsement of the largest denomination. I would opt for God behind me rather than owning the world's largest corporation. God's favor and presence are more valuable than anything else in your life. His favor is a constant reassurance, a source of security amid life's uncertainties.

1 John 4:4 assures us that with God, we have an advantage, stating, "You, dear children, are from God and have overcome them because the one who is in you is greater than the one who is in the world."

If you believe what you have just read, your life will never be the same again. I believe your life is destined for a profound transformation. You will embark on ventures you never thought possible, accomplish feats you never dreamed of, and develop an entirely new perspective on life. You will come to understand that if positive changes can occur for others, they can undoubtedly happen for you, too. This potential for transformation should inspire and motivate you to embrace the changes that God's support can bring into your life.

It is my earnest hope that everyone who has read and believed in this book finds forgiveness for all their sins. Every transgression is pardoned. Now, step into the realm of life with confidence and courage. Don't be afraid to take chances, make choices, and, by faith, anticipate the unfolding of extraordinary blessings in your life like never before.

Finally, I am believing God that good things will start happening for you as never before. It is my prayer that this book has had a profound effect on your mindset and strengthened your faith. So that you will start seeing life through a new lens, say at the start of each day, "I can do all this through Him who gives me strength." Philippians 4:13. Go forth knowing that you are God's child, and that means you are royalty. Your position in this world assures you an advantage, but you have to believe it to receive it. I leave you with the words of Jesus.

John 3:16-17: "For God so loved the world that he gave his one and only Son, that whosoever believes in him should not perish, but have everlasting life. For God did not send his Son into the world to condemn the world, but to save the world through him."

KEY INSIGHTS

Divine Support Enhances Every Aspect of Life: Having God as your ally provides unparalleled support and significantly enhances your chances of achieving happiness, prosperity, health, love, kindness, and peace. Divine support transforms your life, offering reassurance and security amid life's uncertainties, making it more valuable than any worldly endorsement or possession.

Belief in Divine Favor Leads to Transformation: Believing in God's support and favor can lead to profound personal transformation. With God's backing, you can embark on ventures you never thought possible, accomplish feats beyond your dreams, and develop a new perspective on life. Embracing the potential for positive changes inspires motivation and confidence to pursue and realize extraordinary blessings.

Forgiveness and Faith Empower a New Beginning: Embracing forgiveness for past sins and stepping into life with confidence and courage, supported by faith in God's promises, empowers you to take chances and make choices. By starting each day with the affirmation, "I can do all things through Christ who strengthens me," you acknowledge your royal position as God's child, which assures you an advantage in life. Believing in this divine support is crucial to receiving and experiencing the fullness of God's blessings.

Endnotes

Enhance Your Chance of Being Happy

   1. John 3:17 (New King James Version)

Enhance Your Chance of Being Successful

   1. https://www.goodreads.com/quotes/303784-there
-is-a-tide-in-the-affairs-of-men-which

Enhance Your Chance of Having Peace

   1. https://mybible.com/covers/455

Enhance Your Chance of Being Remembered When Your
Life Is Over

   1. https://www.archives.gov/exhibits/featured-docum
ents/emancipation-proclamation#:~:text=President
%20Abraham%20Lincoln%20issued%20the,and%2
0henceforward%20shall%20be%20free.%22

   2. https://www.goodreads.com/quotes/search?q=may
a+angelou+how+it+made+you+feel

Enhance Your Chance of Having Successful Relationships

   1. Matthew 22:37-40 (New King James Version)

   2. https://www.goodreads.com/quotes/574192-if-you
-love-something-set-it-free-if-it-comes

3. Galatians 5:22-23 (New King James Version)

4. https://potentialwithin.wordpress.com/2008/11/1 3/wayne-dyer-on-ego/

5. Ephesians 4:1-3 (New King James Version)

6. Matthew 22:37 (New King James Version)

Enhance Your Chance of Being Saved

1. Acts 16:30-31 (New King James Version)

2. https://hymnary.org/text/he_paid_a_debt_he_did _not_owe

Enhance Your Chance of Living a Longer Life

1. https://en.wikipedia.org/wiki/Job_in_rabbinic_lite rature#:~:text=It%20was%20said%20that%20Job,w hole%20world%20mourned%20Job's%20death

2. *Great is Thy Faithfulness*: Songwriters: Adam Anders / Thomas Chisholm / William Runyan / Great Is Thy Faithfulness lyrics © Tcf Music Publishing Inc, Hill And Range Songs Inc, Every Nation Songcasting

Enhance Your Chance of Being Loved

1. Song of Solomon 8:6 (New King James Version)

2. https://www.goodreads.com/quotes/71281-a-bell-s -not-a-bell-til-you-ring-it--

THE WHITTINGTON HERITAGE EDUCATIONAL ENDOWMENT

A Legacy of Faith and Mission

The Whittington Family has embraced a calling that spans generations—a commitment to nurturing ministry through education and service. Inspired by the lifelong dedication of Rev. A.B. and Gladys Whittington, who served over 50 years in pastoral and evangelistic ministry with the Church of God Organization in Cleveland, Tennessee, the family has established a scholarship endowment. This initiative is designed to honor their legacy and passion for training theological students around the world. The endowed scholarships empower future ministers who are equipped not only to plant churches but also to reach communities with transformative messages of hope.

Embracing the Great Commission

At the heart of this legacy is the enduring mission of the Whittington Heritage Educational Endowment: to make disciples throughout the world by faithfully obeying Christ's Great Commission. As recorded in Matthew 28:19 "Therefore go and make disciples of all nations, baptizing them in the name of the Father and of the Son and of the Holy Spirit. This commitment underpins every aspect of Whittington Heritage Educational Endowment, urging its members to share Christ's love and extend His grace to every corner of the globe.

The Scriptural Foundations

The mission of the Whittington Heritage Educational Endowment is rooted in a rich tapestry of scriptural mandates. Its work is driven by several key purposes:

- Fulfilling the Great Commission

- Sharing Christ's Love

- Ministering to the Totality of Human Need

- Bringing People to the Knowledge of God

- Confessing Christ Boldly

The Practical Mission

Beyond the theological framework, Whittington Heritage Educational Endowment actively implements its vision through a series of dedicated initiatives. The organization is committed to:

- Spreading the gospel of Christ with clarity and conviction.

- Developing mature disciples who can lead and nurture faith within the Kingdom of God.

- Leading non-Christian individuals to salvation through personal and communal outreach.

- Assisting those who are unchurched or only nominally connected to the faith in becoming committed disciples of Christ.

- Training national leaders who can effectively proclaim the gospel within their own communities and across borders.

- Relieving suffering and addressing the practical needs of people in distress.

This comprehensive approach to ministry and mission reflects the same spirit that inspired the Whittington Family. Their scholarship endowment stands as a living legacy—a testament to a heritage of service, education, and unwavering commitment to spreading the transformative love of Christ around the world.

Rev. A.B. and Gladys Whittington

My Dear Friend,

I sincerely hope you will consider supporting the Whittington Heritage Educational Endowment. My parents were rich in faith, though not in worldly wealth. Each week, my mother carefully set aside $2.00 so that when she attended the annual Church of God General Assembly, she could joyfully contribute $100 to missions. Her sacrifice and unwavering dedication left a lasting legacy for her children and grandchildren, serving as a beautiful example of generosity and faith.

Today, through the Whittington Heritage Educational Endowment, we are honored to witness the fruits of the small seed she planted so many years ago.

May God bless you abundantly and keep you and your loved ones in His perfect peace throughout your lives.

Love and prayers,